WESTWARD EXPANSION OF THE UNITED STATES: 1801-1861

by Anita Yasuda

Content Consultant
Dr. Brett Barker
Associate Professor of History
University of Wisconsin–Marathon County

CORE
LIBRARY

Published by ABDO Publishing Company, PO Box 398166, Minneapolis, MN 55439. Copyright © 2014 by Abdo Consulting Group, Inc. International copyrights reserved in all countries. No part of this book may be reproduced in any form without written permission from the publisher. The Core Library™ is a trademark and logo of ABDO Publishing Company.

Printed in the United States of America,
North Mankato, Minnesota
082013
012014

♻ THIS BOOK CONTAINS AT LEAST 10% RECYCLED MATERIALS.

Editor: Jenna Gleisner
Series Designer: Becky Daum

Library of Congress Control Number: 2013945667

Cataloging-in-Publication Data
Yasuda, Anita.
 Westward expansion of the United States: 1801-1861 / Anita Yasuda.
   p. cm. -- (The story of the United States)
Includes bibliographical references and index.
ISBN 978-1-62403-174-8
1. United States--History--19th century--Juvenile literature. 2. United
States--Territorial expansion--History--19th century--Juvenile literature. 3.
Industrial revolution--United States--Juvenile literature. 4. California--Gold
discoveries--Juvenile literature. 5. Slavery--Southern States--History--19th
century--Juvenile literature. 6. United States--Social life and customs--To
1861--Juvenile literature. I. Title.
973.5--dc23

                                                              2013945667

Photo Credits: Bettmann/Corbis/AP Images, cover, 1; North Wind Picture Archives, 4, 16, 18, 20, 22, 25; Alfred R. Waud/Bridgeman Art Library, 8; Jan Arkesteijn, 10; Red Line Editorial, 11, 31; Thomas Mickell Burnham Collection/Bridgeman Art Library, 12, 45; MPI/Getty Images, 15; Peter Newark American Pictures/Bridgeman Art Library, 28, 37; Eric Gay/AP Images, 33; Library of Congress, 34, 39

Cover: Sacagawea guides Lewis and Clark on their journey to explore the West.

CONTENTS

CHAPTER ONE

THE LOUISIANA PURCHASE

In 1801 the third president of the United States took office. His name was Thomas Jefferson. Jefferson was born on April 13, 1743, in Virginia. He was governor of that state for two years, from 1779 to 1781. He then worked as the United States' minister to France, the first US secretary of state, and vice president. Jefferson is best known for writing the Declaration of Independence. This document said

As the nation's new president in 1801, Thomas Jefferson had dreams of expanding the United States.

the United States was a free country and independent from Great Britain.

When Jefferson became president, the United States was much smaller in size. It did not stretch from the Atlantic Ocean to the Pacific Ocean as it does today. It reached north to Canada, south to Florida, and west to the Mississippi River. It was not the only country with land in the region. Beyond the Mississippi River, Great Britain, Spain, and France also claimed large areas of North American land. Native Americans lived here too. Jefferson had dreams of claiming all of this land. He wanted to expand the United States west to the Pacific Ocean.

Port of New Orleans

In 1801 little was known about the land west of the Mississippi River. What Jefferson did know was that there were valuable resources in the West. He also knew that if the country were to grow, it would need the port of New Orleans on the Gulf of Mexico.

Settlers, fur traders, and merchants used the Mississippi River to move their goods to the port of New Orleans. Furs, tobacco, cotton, and sugar were some of the goods shipped from this port. They were sent by boat to towns along the Atlantic coast or to Europe.

New Orleans

In 1717 French explorer Jean-Baptiste Le Moyne de Bienville founded New Orleans in what is now the state of Louisiana. The French chose this area because it was the highest and driest point in the area. Later, with the addition of settlers from France, New Orleans became a thriving city and bustling port.

A Secret Agreement

The French founded New Orleans, but in the 1760s Spain controlled the port. It also controlled the territory west of the Mississippi River to Canada, which was ruled by Great Britain. Spain considered this western land wilderness. Only the port of New Orleans had value to the Spaniards. Spain taxed all goods shipped from the port.

Jefferson knew the United States needed the port of New Orleans in order to trade with other countries and expand westward.

Spain gave the Louisiana Territory, the large area of land west of the Mississippi River, to France in a secret treaty in 1800. By 1801 rumors of this reached the United States. Americans were angry. They worried the French might expand in North America. They also feared the French might cut off access to the Mississippi River. This would harm the US economy and end hope of US growth to the west. Jefferson decided to take action. In 1802 he sent two

envoys to France to buy New Orleans. They were
Robert Livingston and James Monroe.

Negotiations

Livingston and Monroe negotiated with the French,
but they had little success. France's ruler, Napoleon
Bonaparte, had dreams of expanding French control
in North America. But he was busy fighting a series
of wars in Europe. In 1803 Napoleon was ready
to bargain with the
Americans. He needed
more money for his wars.
Napoleon surprised
Jefferson's envoys by
offering to sell them
New Orleans and all of
the Louisiana Territory.
Jefferson's envoys agreed
to the deal.

Robert Livingston

Robert Livingston was Thomas
Jefferson's friend. In 1801
Jefferson made Livingston the
US minister to France. Before
Monroe arrived in France,
Livingston had tried working
out a deal with the French. He
wrote letters and pamphlets.
He even became friends with
Napoleon's brother in an
attempt to reach a deal.

Before Jefferson appointed him US minister to France, Livingston was the first chancellor of New York.

The Louisiana Purchase

On April 30, 1803, the United States and France reached an agreement. The United States paid France $15 million for the Louisiana Territory. This land would become part of 15 states, and it would double the country's size.

The new territory included all land east of the Mississippi River to the Rocky Mountains in the

Louisiana Purchase Land
This map highlights the land the United States acquired after the purchase of the Louisiana Territory in 1803. What do you notice about the area of the Louisiana Purchase? Which states are located in this area today?

west. The United States was now one of the largest countries in the world. But there was a problem. No one knew much about this territory. Before Jefferson could fulfill his dream of expanding the country to the Pacific Ocean, he needed more information about the Louisiana Territory.

EXPLORING THE WEST

In 1803 Jefferson formed a group of men to map the Louisiana Territory and unclaimed territory to the west. They were called the Corps of Discovery. There were many myths about the West. People believed there was a mountain of salt and huge animals, such as the mastodon, living there. Even the president was unsure about what his team would discover in the new territory.

Jefferson appointed Meriwether Lewis and William Clark to lead the Corps of Discovery on their journey to explore the new land to the west.

Jefferson hoped the Corps of Discovery would find a water route to the Pacific Ocean. This passage, known as the Northwest Passage, did not exist. But for centuries explorers had tried to find this route. At that time, nobody knew whether or not it truly existed. If it did, US traders could send goods along it to the coast. They could also use the Northwest Passage to travel to Asia.

The Corps

Two army officers, Meriwether Lewis and William Clark, were in charge of the Corps of Discovery. On May 14, 1804, they left on their adventure to explore the Louisiana Territory. The Corps traveled up the Missouri River on specially

Sacagawea

Sacagawea was a Shoshone Indian. She married a French trapper from Canada named Toussaint Charbonneau, with whom she had a child. Sacagawea and Charbonneau acted as guides and translators for the Corps of Discovery. Sacagawea could speak several Native-American languages. She was able to ask local tribes questions for the Corps. She helped the Corps buy horses and find food.

When Native Americans saw Sacagawea with the Corps, they knew the Corps had come in peace.

built keelboats. The group started out with 33 men. Some were soldiers. Others were frontiersmen who were skilled at living and hunting in the wilderness. Along the way, the Corps grew to include boatmen. Native Americans, including Sacagawea, also joined and acted as translators.

A Successful Journey

Lewis and Clark made notes of everything they saw. They recorded 178 plants and 122 animals. They sent what they called a "barking squirrel," thought to be

In his journal, Clark sketched and wrote about the trout the Corps saw and caught on the expedition.

a prairie dog, to Jefferson. Lewis and Clark made detailed maps and notes about the languages and customs of Native Americans. They met nearly 50 different Native-American tribes during their journey.

On November 15, 1805, Lewis and Clark reached the Pacific Ocean. The 4,200-mile (6,759-km) journey had taken them over land and through water. In their journals, Lewis and Clark wrote of the joy the Corps felt when they heard the roar of the Pacific Ocean.

Trappers and Scouts

Americans were excited about Lewis and Clark's adventures. They too wanted to see the vast plains, towering mountains, and huge forests of the West. Some hoped for riches in the fur trade. Many frontiersmen made the trip west. The US Army, explorers, and settlers used the knowledge the Corps of Discovery explorers gained to guide them westward. Americans were on the move.

Missouri Compromise

After the purchase of the Louisiana Territory, there was a debate in Congress. This new land would create new states. Would the new states be free or slave states? Beginning

Life as a Slave

Slaves did not enjoy freedom like other US citizens. Instead they were forced to work without pay. They worked all day with only short breaks for meals. They were often separated as their families were sold apart. Some slaves worked in their masters' fields. Others, usually women, worked in their owners' homes, cooking, cleaning, and caring for their masters' children.

Slaves in the South were forced to work from sunrise to sunset, often on plantations tending to crops such as cotton.

in the 1600s, African Americans were used as slaves in the United States. Slaves were taken against their will from Africa and brought by ship to America. Here they were forced to work long days in harsh conditions.

By the early 1800s, the North was more industrialized. The South was more rural. Many southern farms relied on slave labor. Northern senators did not want slavery to spread. Southern senators claimed slaves were needed to harvest cotton and other crops. But abolitionists argued slavery was wrong.

By 1820 James Monroe was president. He signed a law called the Missouri Compromise. This law kept balance between slave and free states in Congress. Missouri joined the Union as a slave state, while Maine joined as a free state. In addition, slavery was banned in the northern part of the Louisiana Territory. But the slavery debate was not over.

EXPLORE ONLINE

Chapter Two discusses the Corps of Discovery's adventure in the West and some of Lewis and Clark's discoveries. As you know, every source is different. Visit the Web site below. What additional information did you learn from the Web site? What information was similar to the information in Chapter Two? What information was different?

Lewis and Clark into the Unknown
www.mycorelibrary.com/westward-expansion

CHAPTER THREE

LAND CONFLICTS

Up to the early 1800s, most people in the United States lived along the Atlantic Coast. With the Louisiana Purchase, more and more settlers began moving westward. Native Americans had been living in North America for thousands of years, and many tribes lived in the Louisiana Territory. Each had developed its own language, way of life, and customs.

As more and more settlers moved west, the US government began forcing Native-American tribes off their land.

Most Native Americans joined the British in fighting against Americans during the War of 1812 in hopes of reclaiming their land.

But the new settlers felt it was their right to settle the West.

Native Americans in the War of 1812

In 1812 the United States had declared war on Great Britain, starting the War of 1812. The United States felt Great Britain was trying to limit US trade with other countries. The British navy often searched US ships, taking their cargo and men. The United States also thought Great Britain was encouraging Native Americans to fight with settlers on the frontier.

During the war, many Native Americans fought alongside the British. They hoped the British would help them keep their lands and get back land the United States had already taken. The British promised they would help if the Native Americans helped them defeat the United States. On December 24, 1814, the United States and Great Britain signed the Treaty of Ghent, ending the War of 1812. Land divisions returned to what they were before the war, and the Native Americans were still forced from their land.

Government Policy

Settlers wanted land, and the US government

Sauk Tribe

After the War of 1812, the Sauk tribe was ordered off its lands. The tribe had helped fight against the United States and felt betrayed by the British. In 1832 Chief Black Hawk and the Sauk people tried to return to their land in Illinois, but they were defeated.

listened. During Monroe's presidency, Native Americans were forced to leave states north of the Ohio River. In 1825 the government set aside land just for Native Americans. This area was west of the Mississippi River. It became known as Indian Territory. The government hoped Native Americans would trade their lands in the east for lands in the west. But most tribes did not want to move.

Indian Removal Act

In 1829 Andrew Jackson became president. He told Congress Native Americans were blocking the advances of farmers in the southeast. On May 28, 1830, Jackson proposed the Indian Removal Bill to Congress. Some senators did not agree with the bill. They argued against it, claiming they needed to respect land deals with Native Americans. They said ignoring these deals would reflect poorly on the country.

President Andrew Jackson believed it was necessary to remove Native Americans from their land, resulting in the Indian Removal Act.

Despite debate, the bill passed. It gave the government permission to move Native Americans in the southeast to Indian Territory.

Trail of Tears

The Cherokee was one of the largest tribes in what is now the southeastern United States. They had lived in the Appalachian Mountains for thousands of years. From 1838 to 1839, the US Army forced the Cherokee from their lands. Many had no time to gather their belongings, such as blankets and food. The sick, elderly, or weak rode in wagons, while the others walked. Approximately 17,000 Cherokee were forced to leave their homelands for western Arkansas and eastern Oklahoma. Their march was 800 miles (1,287 km) long. More than 4,000 people died on the way, earning the march the name "The Trail of Tears."

Seminole Native Americans

The Indian Removal Act also affected the Seminole tribe of Florida. In 1819 Spain sold Florida to the United States. Between 1835 and 1842, the US Army removed 3,000 Seminole to Indian Territory. Some Seminole escaped to the Florida swamps. From there they continued to fight the US Army. The Seminole never surrendered.

Private soldier John G. Burnett of the US Army helped remove the Cherokee from their land. In this letter, he recalls what he saw during the Trail of Tears:

I saw the helpless Cherokees arrested and dragged from their homes, and driven at the bayonet point into the stockades. And in the chill of a drizzling rain . . . I saw them loaded like cattle or sheep into six hundred and forty-five wagons and started toward the west.

One can never forget the sadness and solemnity of that morning. Chief John Ross led in prayer and when the bugle sounded and the wagons started rolling many of the children rose to their feet and waved their little hands good-by to their mountain homes, knowing they were leaving them forever. Many of these helpless people did not have blankets and many of them had been driven from home barefooted.

Source: *"A Soldier Recalls the Trail of Tears."* Learn NC: North Carolina in the New Nation. *Learn NC, n.d. Web. Accessed June 1, 2013.*

Changing Minds

Imagine what a Cherokee might have to say about the same events. Write a letter expressing the Cherokee's point of view. How might this person have felt about being forced from home?

CHAPTER FOUR

MANIFEST DESTINY

Before 1840 there were few settlers in the Pacific Northwest. California and much of the West belonged to Mexico, which became independent from Spain in 1821. Many Americans believed the United States should settle the western lands. Some people felt it was their destiny or that God wanted them to move to the West. This belief was known as Manifest Destiny.

In the early 1840s, thousands of settlers moved west using the Oregon Trail, which often presented rough land and waterways to cross.

The president in the late 1840s, James K. Polk, was in favor of westward expansion. Polk believed the country should stretch from coast to coast. He wanted the United States to include Texas, California, and the Oregon Territory, along the northern Pacific Coast.

The Great Migration

In 1843, 1,000 pioneers journeyed west using a route known as the Oregon Trail. This 2,000-mile (3,219-km) journey became known as "The Great Migration." At the time, the Oregon Territory was not part of the United States. Stories of rich soil and a mild climate drew people to the Oregon Territory. Water was plentiful in this part of the country. It was

Mormon Movement

People moved west for many reasons. Some, such as the Mormons, a religious group, hoped to find a place where they could practice their religion peacefully. In 1846 nearly 5,000 Mormons and their leader, Brigham Young, followed the Oregon Trail west. In 1847 they reached the Great Salt Lake area of Utah and decided to settle there.

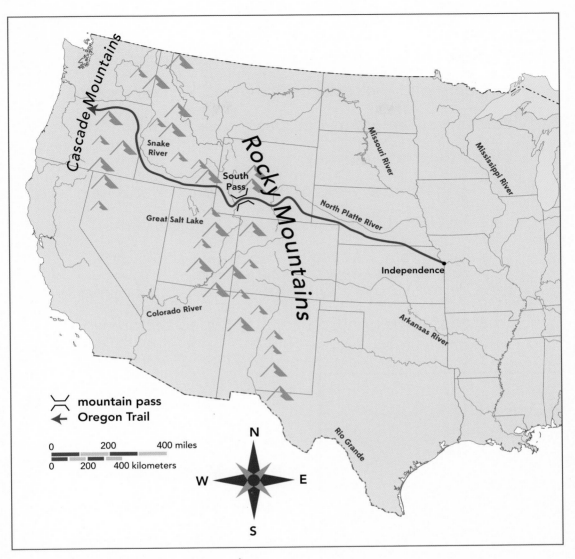

Oregon Trail

After stocking up on supplies in Independence, Missouri, pioneers headed west. This map shows some of the major landmarks settlers may have passed on their journey west. Look at the map and imagine making this trip. Write 200 words about what you saw and how you felt on the journey.

an ideal place for lumber mills and flour mills. The pioneers who took part in The Great Migration called themselves emigrants because they left the United States for a new territory.

In 1846, after years of negotiation, Great Britain and the United States signed the Oregon Treaty. This agreement said the two countries would split the Oregon Country. On August 14, 1848, Congress created the Oregon Country. It included the present-day states of Oregon, Idaho, Washington, and western Montana.

Battle of the Alamo

One of the most famous battles of the Texas Revolution was the Battle of the Alamo. The Alamo was an abandoned Spanish church the Texans used as a fort. Here 187 Texans fought against 5,000 Mexican troops. The Texan soldiers all died, but approximately 20 Texan women and children survived.

The Mexican-American War

During the early 1800s, many Americans migrated to Texas. Texas was part of Mexico at the time. Texas declared its independence from Mexico, but Mexico

The Alamo, the site of the Battle of the Alamo during the Texas Revolution, still stands today and is a popular tourist attraction in San Antonio, Texas.

did not agree with this act. US settlers fought a series of battles with Mexico from 1835 to 1836. These battles are known as the Texas Revolution.

From 1846 to 1848, the Unites States and Mexico were at war. On February 2, 1848, the two countries signed the Treaty of Guadalupe Hidalgo, ending the war. The United States won, taking ownership of more than 500,000 square miles (1,294,994 sq km) of new territory. This area became California, Arizona, New Mexico, Texas, and parts of Utah, Colorado, Nevada, and Wyoming.

GOLD RUSH

On January 24, 1848, James Marshall found gold at Sutter's Mill near Sacramento, California. Newspaper headlines read, "Gold on the American River!" Soon trading ships brought news of the gold to countries around the world.

On December 5, 1848, Polk confirmed gold had been found in California. At that time, only 14,000 non-Native Americans lived there. Talk of gold

James Marshall stands in front of Sutter's Mill in California, where he first discovered gold in 1848.

inspired 90,000 people to move to California in 1849. They were nicknamed the "forty-niners." Some were US farmers, soldiers, and merchants. Many crossed the plains on foot. Others took clipper ships. The voyage took between 150 and 200 days by sea.

Miners from Around the World

People came from around the world to look for gold. When word of California's gold rush reached China, many people became determined to get there. At that time in China, people were starving. Once they arrived in California, most never found gold. Chinese miners faced prejudice. They were chased away or had to work land other miners had already mined.

Foreign Miners License Law

In 1850 the California legislature passed the Foreign Miners License Law. Miners who were not US citizens were charged $20 per month. Many Chinese miners could not afford to pay the fee and left the gold fields. Some started businesses in San Francisco. Others went to work on the railroad.

Gold prospectors from Ireland search for gold in 1849.

Slavery

In 1850 California joined the Union as a free state. Approximately 200 to 300 slaves came to work in the gold fields during the gold rush. Some found gold and were able to buy their freedom. But when the Fugitive Slave Law of 1850 passed, many African Americans feared they would have to return to their lives as slaves. The act said it was illegal for slaves to flee a master even if they were in a free state, such as California. Private citizens were required to help capture former slaves. The act also made it illegal to

Slavery Sparks the American Civil War

Tensions continued to grow in the United States between people who wanted to use slave labor and people who felt keeping slaves was wrong. Then on April 12, 1861, the two sides collided at Fort Sumter in Charleston, South Carolina. Confederate troops from the South fired on Union troops occupying Fort Sumter. The American Civil War (1861–1865) had begun. It would continue for the next four years.

hide slaves. People caught helping slaves were jailed or fined.

Homestead Act

The gold rush reached its peak in 1852. Many people stayed in California. Some people didn't have enough money to travel back to their homes. Others opened businesses or started farms and ranches.

Pioneers during the 1840s and the 1850s rarely settled on the land east of the Rocky Mountains. This land was called the Great Plains. The plains had few trees, little rain, and bad storms. People did not believe they could live there. Instead they journeyed to the West Coast.

The first homestead under the Homestead Act was in Gage County, Nebraska.

To encourage more people to settle on the plains, President Abraham Lincoln signed the Homestead Act in 1862. The act gave 160 acres (65 ha) of free land to qualified settlers. Settlers had to be 21 years of age or older, and they had to be a US citizen or intend to become one. People had to agree to build a home and stay on the land for five years. Thousands of people wanted free land. They packed all of their belongings and moved west.

Life on the plains was difficult. There were fires, droughts, and locusts. But settlers stayed because of the rich farmland, and the nation grew. In 1800 there were approximately 5 million people living in the United States. By 1861, 31 million people lived in the country. Immigrants continued to flock to the United States from Europe throughout the 1800s. In addition there were new states and territories. What started in 1801 as a dream of westward expansion ended 60 years later with a nation stretching from coast to coast.

FURTHER EVIDENCE

Chapter Five discusses prejudice minorities faced during the gold rush. Go to the Web site below and read excerpts from Mifflin Wistar Gibbs's autobiography *Shadow and Light*. Gibbs was the first elected African-American municipal court judge and an important abolitionist. In 1855 he organized the First State Convention of Colored Citizens of California to fight for equal rights. Take notes as you read the first few paragraphs of Gibbs's story. Do your notes support the information in Chapter Five?

Mifflin Wistar Gibbs's Autobiography

www.mycorelibrary.com/westward-expansion

In 1849 Edward Jackson left Massachusetts for California to find gold. He kept a diary as he traveled. In this passage, Jackson writes about the grim realities of the trip:

One of our axle trees broke which detained us & compelled us to reverence the day [Sunday]. At this place are the graves of two emigrants who died the past week. O do not leave my bones here. If possible let them lay at home—if not, let it be California. The idea of the plains is horrible! I now see my journey in its true light and if I am permitted to record, the pages of my journal will tell a fearful tale.

Source: *"Trails to Utah and the Pacific: Diaries and Letters, 1846–1869."* The Library of Congress: American Memory. *Web. Accessed July 3, 2013.*

Consider Your Audience

Review this passage closely. Imagine you are part of the same group heading to California. To keep your parents from worrying, how would you rewrite this information to make the trip sound more positive? Create a letter, writing the same information for your new audience.

IMPORTANT DATES

1801

Thomas Jefferson becomes the third president of the United States.

1803

The United States purchases Louisiana from France for $15 million.

1804

Meriwether Lewis and William Clark embark on an expedition from Saint Louis, Missouri, to the Pacific Ocean on May 14.

1846

The United States and Great Britain sign the Oregon Treaty, agreeing to split Oregon.

1847

Mormon Brigham Young and his followers reach the Great Salt Lake area of Utah and settle.

1848

James Marshall discovers gold at Sutter's Mill near Sacramento, California, on January 24.

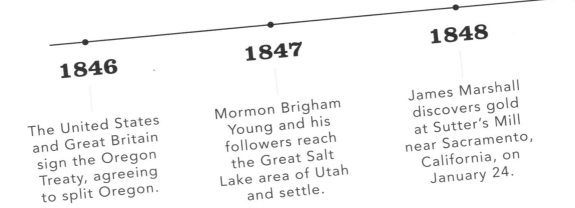

1812

The US Congress declares war against Great Britain.

1814

The War of 1812 ends on December 24 when the United States and Great Britain sign the Treaty of Ghent.

1838–1839

The Cherokee are forced to leave their land for Indian Territory on a journey later called the Trail of Tears.

1848

The United States and Mexico end the Mexican-American War with the signing of the Treaty of Guadalupe Hidalgo on February 2.

1861

The Civil War begins with the battle at Fort Sumter on April 12, 1861.

1862

President Abraham Lincoln signs the Homestead Act, giving free land to settlers and encouraging white settlers to inhabit the Great Plains.

Say What?

Studying the westward expansion of the United States can mean learning a lot of new vocabulary. Find five words in this book you have never seen or heard before. Use a dictionary to find out what they mean. Then write each meaning in your own words, and use each word in a sentence.

Why Do I Care?

Can you find similarities between your life and the life of the early settlers discussed in this book? How did the role US pioneers played in settling the West affect your life today? How might your life be different if the United States had never expanded its western border to the Pacific Ocean?

Surprise Me

Chapter One discusses the Louisiana Purchase. After reading this book, what two or three facts about the purchase did you find most surprising? Write a few sentences about each fact. Why did you find them surprising?

Tell the Tale

Chapter Three in this book discusses the Trail of Tears. Write 200 words explaining the Cherokees' journey to Indian Territory. Describe why they were moved and how they got to Indian Territory. Be sure to set the scene, develop a sequence of events, and write a conclusion.

GLOSSARY

abolitionist
a person in favor of ending slavery

clipper
a fast sailing ship with three masts

emigrant
a person who settles in a new area within his or her own country or in another country

envoy
a messenger sent from one country to another

gold rush
a large movement of people to an area with gold

homestead
a piece of land on which people farm and build homes

industrialized
made up of factories that produce large amounts of products and employ many workers

keelboat
a boat used mostly for moving freight on a river

mastodon
a large, extinct mammal that resembled an elephant

pioneer
one of the first people to explore a new area

prospector
a person looking for gold or other valuable minerals

LEARN MORE

Books

Berne, Emma Carlson. *Crossing the Continent with Lewis & Clark*. New York: Sterling, 2010.

Lusted, Marcia Amidon. *The Oregon Trail*. Edina, MN: ABDO, 2012.

Zurn, Jon. *The Louisiana Purchase*. Edina, MN: ABDO, 2008.

Web Links

To learn more about westward expansion, visit ABDO Publishing Company online at **www.abdopublishing.com**. Web sites about westward expansion are featured on our Book Links page. These links are routinely monitored and updated to provide the most current information available.

Visit **www.mycorelibrary.com** for free additional tools for teachers and students.

INDEX

ABOUT THE AUTHOR

Anita Yasuda is the author of more than 60 books for children. She enjoys writing biographies, books about science and social studies, and chapter books. Anita lives with her family and dog in Huntington Beach, California.